T0380816

Praise for *How to Meditate with Jesus*

"The author's blend of biblical understanding with her unique interpretation of functional meditation is unlike anything I've seen on the subject. Seeing meditation through Tonyah's personal lens helped me view my practice in a new light. I highly recommend this book to anyone looking to start a meditation practice or advance their current practice to a higher level."

—Delphine Channels, founder of ThinkCoach

"Meditating with Jesus brings the teachings we all value—love, peace, joy—into a living reality we can all experience through a beautiful daily practice. Tonyah shares all she has learned from her journey of pain, recovery, and healing to find the light, weaving it into a gift that will benefit all who use it."

—G. Khalsa, emotions coach and author

"Learn to love yourself, others, and your life through this very well-designed and gentle guide to transformation through a meditation practice of discovery, vulnerability, healing, and inward peace. Tonyah has created a process that is incredibly inviting and inspiring."

—Leslie Calhoun, Optivest Wealth Management

"Divinely inspired, beautifully written, and filled with personal experience and insight. Tonyah has written a wonderful guide for anyone seeking to deepen their connection to and experience of God through Jesus."

—Steve Sanders, master meditation teacher

"Tonya writes with a heart full of wonder for Jesus combined with the practical and powerful experience of meditation. Her passion in this book to share the spiritual practice of How to Meditate With Jesus is contagious as you learn new tools to bring to your own life."

—Arianna Caligiuri, MS spiritual director, coach, and consultant

"You have a warm, relatable style of writing, which allows readers to connect with your text on a deep level. Your honest transparency about each step in your testimony will encourage others who may be experiencing similar situations. By bringing forward the benefits of meditation, including restoration, harmony, connection, and more, your prayer journal leads readers to stay mindful of their spiritual needs, and to stay aligned with God's virtues that restore us. We appreciate the inclusion of faith statements throughout, as it is apparent that the Lord has renewed your Spirit, and you are hopeful to share this with others."

—Anonymous

"Daily time with God is the most important thing we can do in our lives. The transforming power of godly meditation is something everyone is in need of. I love how Tonyah has given clear steps to take for those who are just beginning as well as stirring a deeper hunger for those who may be more practiced. I love the doodle drawings which will allow one to slow down and color as the Holy Spirit speaks to them. This is a must read for anyone seeking a deeper connection with God."

—La Vonne Earl, author, *A Coach for Christ*

"Tonyah Dee's book was SO inspirational for me!!! I have struggled with meditation from the beginning and always felt that I was 'faking it.' Her beautifully written book has made me recommit to try again. THANK YOU, Tonyah!"

—Pam Patterson, Esq.

"Tonyah has conceived and crafted a book that is as functional as it is inspiring and motivational. Presented clearly and faithfully, the stories, principles, and lessons collectively represent a valuable emotional toolbox that is as relevant to longtime believers as it is to newcomers. All are welcome here."

—Chris Epting, author

HOW TO MEDITATE WITH JESUS

EIGHT STEPS TO
CONNECT TO A HIGHER POWER
AND
BE SET FREE

(INCLUDES A FORTY-DAY WORKBOOK, JOURNAL, AND DOODLE ART)

written and
illustrated by
Tonyah DEE

WestBow
PRESS®
A DIVISION OF THOMAS NELSON
& ZONDERVAN

www.yahlight.com

WestBow Press books may be ordered through booksellers or by contacting:

WestBow Press
A Division of Thomas Nelson & Zondervan
1663 Liberty Drive
Bloomington, IN 47403
www.westbowpress.com
844-714-3454

Illustrations by Tonyah Dee

ISBN: 979-8-3850-1106-3 (sc)
ISBN: 979-8-3850-1107-0 (e)

Print information available on the last page.

WestBow Press rev. date: 04/02/2024

To Human Beings

I am, you are, he is, she is, we are, they are—joined imperfectly together as one.
When we meditate with Jesus, we discover and recover our true nature, helping
us to recognize the true nature of others. I hope this book helps humans
to become more like Jesus, able to give love and receive God's love.

CONTENTS

PART 1: HOW TO MEDITATE WITH JESUS...xi

Preface 1

Acknowledgments 7

Introduction 11

Step 1: Daily Practice—Restore 23

Step 2: The Body—Sanctuary 33

Step 3: The Breath—Create 45

Step 4: The Word—Harmonize 57

Step 5: The Spirit—Connect 69

Step 6: The Heart—Open 81

Step 7: The Soul—Renew 93

Step 8: Prayer—Believe 107

Conclusion 119

PART 2: MEDITATE WITH JESUS 131

8-Step Daily Practice..133

Cheat Sheet 135

40-DAY MEDITATION AND PRAYER JOURNAL 141

Afterword.. 190

Appendix: Resources for Your Daily Practice.................................... 193

Notes 195

Bibliography.. 199

PART ONE

HOW TO MEDITATE WITH JESUS

PREFACE

I thought I was done writing this book when I handed the manuscript over to Pastor Robert Schuller of Robert Schuller Ministries for review.

"Consider sharing your theology with your reader," he kindly suggested.

So, here I am sharing my faith walk and beliefs with you. By sharing my theology and journey, I hope you will feel a call like I did to get to know this person called Jesus Christ. If you already know him, then perhaps you desire to go deeper into your heart to discover how unconditional loving our God really is. Either way, if you follow the steps in this workbook, you can experience how powerful God's light is at dissolving darkness and bringing you new life right now.

Several years ago, I was so desperate to get rid of the darkness in my life that I committed to meet with God every day. It was through spending time surrendering to God's power and his light and love that I healed a bunch of poor coping mechanisms stemming from my childhood.

"God is good, and God is great, and we thank him for our food. Amen."

That simple prayer was the only exposure I had to religion in my youth. I didn't go to church. I didn't read the Bible. I had no formal exposure to religion except for the simple prayer my family would say before every meal.

And you know what? That prayer was enough—more than enough—to launch a solid faith walk throughout my life and become the foundation of my theology:

I know I love God. And I know I am loved by God. And I am thankful.

This simple yet profound belief I formed as a child has helped me to see the good in everything and everyone.

It taught me the value of gratitude and the ability to say amen to everything that happens in my life.

At twenty-four, I invited Jesus into my heart and have made studying scriptural texts from around the world one of my life's callings. However, it was the Bible that gave me the most insight and direction toward the path of freedom, and it spoke to me clearly and deeply.

Through studying the Bible, praying, learning from the experience of others, and practicing listening and observation daily, I have expanded my theology while always coming back to the core truth that God is good. God is great. And we thank him.

I can best succinctly describe my spiritual beliefs, my theology, through the following Bible verses that speak the truth to me. Most of us have some belief about spiritual matters, even if we declare to have none, which is a belief in itself. I invite you to try meditating with Jesus and have an openness and willingness to form new beliefs. Many spiritual truths exist around the world and in many religions, and I believe they all lead to God eventually. These are some that led me into a deeper relationship with the Creator of all things.

I believe we are body, soul, and spirit (1 Thessalonians 5:23 NIV); that we are all born with a spark of divine light in our spirits (Proverbs 20:27 NIV); and that we are connected to God, who is spirit (John 4:24 NIV). This light in humans is the light of Christ (John 1:4 NIV).

I believe we are all created in God's image (Genesis 1:27 NIV), God is light, and in him is no darkness at all (1 John 1:5 NIV). God is over all, through all, and in all (Ephesians 4:6 NIV). I believe we can learn to be still and know God (Psalm 46:10 NIV). God's spirit is poured out into our hearts like it was in Jesus (Romans 5:5 NIV).

I believe Jesus was who he said he was. He is the Son of Man (John 6:53 NIV), and he brought us the good news of how to be set free through spiritual illumination (Luke 4:43 NIV).

Jesus came to give light and enlighten everyone (John 1:9 NIV). I believe that Jesus is the Word (John 1:1–3, 1:14 NIV); and his words show us how to find the eternal love, life, and light of God.

His words can change the way we think, and since our thoughts can lead to emotions and then to actions, meditating with Jesus can transform our lives. Renew our hearts. Jesus teaches us how to keep our hearts open so the love and life of God can gracefully flow in and out.

I believe we can find the power that we seek in the spirit of God. Jesus leads us to God and his Holy Spirit (John 3:5–6 NIV).

I believe Christ, his life and light, is in everyone and every living thing in creation (John 1:1–4 NIV).

I believe we can ignite and empower this light when we ask for it, seek it, find it, receive it, believe it, listen to it, and then follow it.

There you go. These scripture verses convey my theology. Forming our own beliefs about spirituality is a process. It has taken me many years and many paths. We are given free will to explore and discover for ourselves our own theology. I'm not suggesting that mine needs to be yours, but that the exploring of another's truth can be helpful when defining your own beliefs. Everyone has their own, so let no preconceived notions or fears you have about the Bible, God, Jesus, or even meditation get in the way of igniting the light within and leading you to your authentic truth.

After so much searching throughout my entire life, I have not found a more dynamic way to ask, seek, find, and receive this powerful source of light than through scripture and Christ-centered meditation and prayer.

That is why I wrote this book and why I feel so passionate about helping others learn how to create a practice of meditation and prayer for themselves.

There is a power that can be used for light or darkness, good or evil. My goal is to claim this meditation and prayer practice in the name of the sovereign power of Christ, hoping you will connect to the power that is "good." This will lead you to freedom! And in that freedom, you will have the power to dissolve any darkness.

This practice should help you grow these inner virtues: peace, patience, kindness, goodness, faithfulness, self-control, joy, and the ability to love. You will grow closer to God, and it will change your life so you can experience more happiness and power.

I believe we can accomplish these goals by meeting with God every day for at least a season. During this period, we can learn to befriend our souls and surrender them to God's powerful spirit, which will then guide our lives into areas that satisfy our souls. We can learn to discern between the voice of our souls and that of God's spirit. This enables us to decrease self-sabotage and empower an internal guidance system that leads us toward the good.

Meditating with Jesus can help you know God and your unique and authentic soul.

This is the opposite of a meditation practice that may ask you to ignore, avoid, empty, or deny God or requires you to idolize a person other than God. In this practice, I want you to draw upon the powers of the living God, not just the power in your soul. It is not about increasing ego strength; it's about calming the ego down so we can surrender to a more powerful source than ourselves.

Like Jesus, I believe in inclusivity, equality, and social justice. There is no one way or thing you must do or say to receive God because God is already within you.

The only requirement is to believe in Jesus and recognize the life and light of Christ inside you. Jesus wants you to know how to ignite and empower that light to receive the fullness of all that God is. Only then can you know and understand without a doubt that you are a child of God.

Jesus asks of us, "Love the Lord your God with all your heart and with all your soul and with all your mind" (Matthew 22:37 NIV). This is the first and greatest commandment. The second is like it: "Love your neighbor as yourself" (Mark 12:31 NIV). If you master this, everything else will fall into place.

You will learn to love staying connected to this divine union, which can bring you more benefits than you could ever imagine.

Now, I'm sure someone out there may be wondering who do I think I am to teach such a powerful, spiritual, yet scientific practice. Well, for starters, I have a bachelor's degree in science and administrative dietetics and have done extensive research. But what qualifies me the most to write this book is the deep belief I hold in all the empirical evidence that supports the astounding benefits of light, stillness, breath, sound, heart coherence, meditation, and prayer.

As a child of God, I've been given an authentic calling because God's spirit is alive in me and working through me in a unique new way to bring internal and external harmony and goodness to those who will believe or at least try what I teach in this book.

I invite you to learn how to meditate with Jesus. Come as you are and meditate on God's glory, mercy, beauty, and creation. And always remember . . .

God is good. God is great. And we thank him.

Amen and hallelujah.

ACKNOWLEDGMENTS

First, I sincerely thank my only son, Matthew, for the blessing of being your mother. You, my beloved son, have been my biggest inspiration to become a better person. I have learned how to love unconditionally because when I see you, I understand that there is no other way. I hope I taught you by example how to forgive and love people and continue to pursue your divine purpose.

Thank you to my father for demonstrating to me how to live a joyful life and not judge people but see the good in them and for reading or listening to everything I produced along the way. To my mother, who said to me too many times to count, "Be empowered." To my stepmother, who is "more like me" and has taught me to embrace life, love others, and follow the dreams placed in my heart.

Thank you to my ex-husband, who became the impetus for me to learn how to meditate with Jesus.

Thank you to all my amazing girlfriends who have supported me on my journey and have been my sisters. To Jane, Donna, Arianna, Julia, Hari, and Marie for helping to put this book and other YahLight projects together.

Thank you to Steve Sanders for teaching me to meditate and G. Khalsa for teaching me how to embrace my emotions. And a big thank you to Marty Rifkin, who brings to life the songs, meditations, and contemplations stored in my heart out to the world on magical musical notes.

Thank you to John, my brother in Christ, for your musical talents, for always challenging me to understand Jesus and the Bible better, and for being the caretaker of the kingdom.

Thank you to Pastor Rick Warren and your wife, Kay. It is who you both are as much as what you teach that inspires me daily to surrender my soul to God's infinite love and remain on the path of my divine purpose.

And a very big thank you to Stacey Freeman, editor and writer. Without your help, this book, my stories, and my other books to come would have remained in the dark. You are an angel from God, and that, I believe, is how it works.

INTRODUCTION

[O]ne God and Father of all, who is over all and through all and in all.
—Ephesians 4:6 NIV

You've probably heard about some of the many benefits that can come from meditation. For starters, meditation can increase self-awareness, promote well-being,[1] and cleanse your heart, allowing you to reach higher states of clarity and consciousness. It can help you focus your energy, so you can make positive changes in your life, including breaking bad habits, which will make you more productive. As you will see, meditation can, in a broader sense, enable you to become a better person—the person you are meant to be.

Meditating with Jesus specifically can offer you an additional benefit you may not have heard of: it can deepen your faith and understanding of God. As you will learn in this book, such spiritual "enlightenment," an expansion of *inner* light, can further improve your life in ways you've never imagined.

Through a Christ-centered meditation practice, you can experience what it means to be embodied, where, within your body, your soul and spirit are united with God's spirit. This alert sense of presence, the powerful aliveness that exists inside, empowers you to think more like Jesus, *become* more like Jesus, and love as Jesus loved. From this perspective, you will gain more insight into who you are and, more importantly, who you are meant to be. The common thread? You need to go inside yourself to your heart where God lives.

The more you practice, and the more serious you are about the practice, the more you will likely notice that you're behaving differently. Those who know you will probably see it too. That's because you will be cocreating with God, whose goal is to lead you down a path toward your unique, authentic life, one full of meaning and purpose. As you travel down this path, your heart will transform into one that is open, cleansed, and pure, allowing you to stay present in the flow of life.

Jesus meditated with, prayed to, and called out to his Abba Father (Mark 14:36 NIV). Now, before I go further, I want to explain one important point underlying much of the writing in this workbook: even though Jesus called God Abba Father, linguistic authorities in the language Jesus spoke at the time, Aramaic, tell us he did so to emphasize the invitation, the choice, we all have, irrespective of gender, to develop a close and caring relationship with the Creator of All.[2]

Calling God the endearing term *father* symbolizes the potential for direct one-on-one communication with a loving and compassionate presence. Using the word *abba* makes the meaning of *father* (as it pertains to God) even more intimate. *Abba* is another word for *father*, like *daddy* or *papa*. However, unlike a human father, Abba Father is our good and divine parent, who is full of love and concern and longs for a relationship with all humans. Jesus demonstrated that he clearly made the choice to love God back as a child naturally does with a loving parent.

In the Bible and this workbook, God the Father is referred to as a male figure. However, as we can intuit, the Creator of All, our beloved parent, is genderless.[3] God the spirit has existed from the beginning of time. You may be more comfortable or know this divine beloved presence by one of many names. Whatever name you use, one thing remains certain: the one known by many names is always calling to you.

When meditating, you can hear that voice better. That's because, during meditation, you go inward to your heart, where God's spirit is living. There, you cultivate the virtues of stillness, self-control, and peace, which allows you to recover and restore inner power. This inexhaustible source of power is accessible to everyone. The more we tap into it, the better we understand it. God is always sending us messages, relaying signals, and shining his infinite love and intelligence to everyone. Our task is to call back.

As this relationship becomes more established, you may no longer need outer fixes like substances or materialism to fill a void or make yourself feel better. Instead, you become better at pushing those distractions aside because being filled with spiritual power brings you more joy than these fixes ever could.

Through Christ-centered meditation, you learn to lift the veil and look with compassion at the injuries and struggles of your soul. This is what God wants. God's spirit is within you to provide safety, comfort, counsel, and help. He guides you with his voice and light through all forms of darkness. As he does, your heart can heal and become lighter. Self-love can grow. Seeking, finding, and believing in God, his spirit, and the love of Jesus can, therefore, bring renewed energy to your body, soul, and spirit.

Sounds great, right? Well, the best part is yet to come. In the following chapters, I have outlined the path to improving your life. Every chapter represents a step, one of the eight higher powers we all possess, to get closer to God, the highest power. These eight powers are daily practice, the body, the breath, the word, the spirit, the heart, the soul, and prayer.

As you will discover, meditating with Jesus is simple yet takes practice. After reading this workbook and completing the exercises in it, you will have the tools to tap into the capacity for transformation already in you. God designed you as a supernatural, divine human. However, sometimes, inside and outside forces can drown out your God-given power. That's why the goal of Christ-centered meditation is to "be still" so you can get to know God (Psalm 46:10 NIV). You will also get to know who you are, which includes your unique soul and true self.

The process is simple, so anyone can learn how to do it. A meditation session can look something like this: you start by becoming still, slowly and consciously taking in the breath of life. I like to begin worshipping by singing a devotional chant or a hymn, but you don't have to. When I sing, I feel the sound's vibration penetrating my every cell and the harmony in my body expanding. But everyone's experience is different. The point is to center yourself. Once you relax, close your eyes and meditate.

You may be thinking, *What exactly does that mean?* Well, when you meditate, you come to a secret place, the realm of God, a place of harmony and understanding. There, you open your heart so that God can cleanse it. You surrender your soul to a higher power so that God may heal it. You connect to the light, life, and love of Christ, allowing you to become lighter and more peaceful. As Jesus said, "I am the light of the world. Whoever follows me will never walk in darkness, but will have the light of life" (John 8:12 NIV). Through Christ-centered meditation, you can be liberated from the darkness.

This can result in an interior spaciousness where happiness, hope, and joy can expand and fill the body. It is a place you can return to whenever you need to. It is a place where heaven and earth, divinity and humanity, are in harmony and where you can be too. Meditation allows you to go from the outer world inward to your heart and soul to explore who you are. The goal is to listen and then surrender it all, settling into God's spirit and truth and finding light and grace within.

Once you feel satisfied and receptive, you can end in prayer, becoming thankful, admitting struggles, and asking God for what you need. You give him your heart, and he gives his back. What you can receive from meditation is synchronization toward peacefulness, compassion, and love. You need not earn these things. Just accept them. These virtues are already within you.

INTROSPECTION

Ever since I was a teenager, I've vacillated between eating jars of peanut butter and running like Forrest Gump. I've suffered from anxiety and periods of depression. It was confusing and stressful. I'd eventually become a registered dietitian, an expert on the needs of the physical body, to gain self-control. But that didn't give me the peace I was searching for. Even after years of soul-searching in psychotherapy, I still couldn't shake the stream of fear and worry that plagued me.

For many years, I read self-help books, attended personal-growth workshops and Bible studies, and continued to run in search of answers. I acquired various certifications and even completed an eight-year meditation training. While all these things helped, I wasn't completely satisfied. Something in my life was still missing.

After decades of relentlessly searching for a solution to improve my health and happiness, I finally found it while meditating early one morning. I heard God's voice, and my life changed. That was the moment I awakened to Christ's presence within me. A light inside me began glowing, and I ceased striving. Slowing down, I learned to sit in my body, found my soul, and surrendered to the unconditional love of God.

One of the most beneficial lessons I've learned from meditating with Jesus is how to communicate with God. I've learned to talk and listen. There have been so many times when I was rescued from my suffering simply because I heard God's voice.

Even now, God continues to lead me out of the darkness and into the light. I speak honestly to him; and he guides, counsels, and helps me find a deeper truth, a larger perspective that lights the path ahead and allows me to walk in a natural rhythm. This is the story of how I saved and improved my life through Christ-centered meditation and prayer, and nothing brings me more satisfaction than sharing it with you and the world.

INSIGHT

Exploring our inner life can be daunting but necessary for growth. After all, how can we become our best selves and live peaceful lives if we don't know who we are? Self-awareness is the beginning of wisdom. A part of our personal work is to know the perceptions, mindsets, thoughts, beliefs, feelings, and rudimentary desires that determine our view of reality and, therefore, help us to understand how we can color and create the reality we live in.

Holding on to our old and comfortable ways of being can cause resistance to change or prevent us from moving into higher levels of functioning and new ways of being. Instead, we must be willing to explore what keeps us stagnant or what blocks us from achieving greater happiness. Meditation is self-discovery. It's an exploration of one's soul and an excavation and cleansing of our minds' perspective.

Initiating and allowing a change in perspective is essential. Without this, we can get stuck in the same paradigm—in the same habits, thoughts, emotions, and desires—that prohibits us from recovering our power and growing into who we are meant to be. Unfortunately, we are all resistant to changing and exploring concepts we don't believe in, support, or understand.

However, note that resistance can come up because there might be something important for us to do, look at, or learn. We might need to make a change, and change is often hard. It can require courage and soul-searching. Perhaps the most difficult aspect of meditation is overcoming the resistance to do it.

In knowing this, we also need to know that resistance *can* point the way to our souls' truth, evolution, purpose, and divine calling. Meditation is a discovery of these gifts. By resisting insight or change, we may be resisting getting to know our souls and the messages inside our hearts. Our "free" will (free in that we make choices for ourselves daily) can be defiant, rebellious, and powerful, directing us away from the very thing that might benefit us. Inner work allows us to explore the truth beyond resistance, and Christ-centered meditation is effective for doing that work.

All adult humans are on a path of recovery. We can lose contact with precious pieces of our identity. Recovery is searching for and finding something lost and regaining possession or control of something missing, stolen, or buried. It is a return to optimal health, mind, or strength.[4] Every day, during meditation, we are given the gift of recovering what we lost during the years prior or the day before. Maybe it was peace or happiness. Maybe it was self-control or innocence. Regardless, we recover what we lost along the way. We become awake to who we are and the beauty in and around us.

INSPIRATION

Learning to meditate with Jesus keeps us tethered to inner transformation. Every time we return to this space, we become less resistant than the time before it. With practice, we feel an intimate alignment with our multidimensional nature: our body, soul, and spirit. We grow in our ability to love and remain calm, even during hard times. Instead of seeking rewards from the outside world, we find the spiritual world within nurturing and satisfying. A balance between the material and the spiritual world brings layers of unity, harmony, wholeness, and abundance into our lives.

This eight-step Christ-centered meditation and prayer practice intends to surrender our souls and connect our spirits to God's. The motive is to be consciously led by the spirit of God.

We are so much more than the anxiety, the addiction, the fluctuating thoughts of the mind, the waves of feelings, and the impulsive behaviors that come and go. We can choose to be guided and given power on our path to our divine authentic purpose. The eleventh step of Alcoholics Anonymous (AA) states it perfectly: "[We] [s]ought through prayer and meditation to improve our conscious contact with God as we understood Him, praying only for knowledge of His will for us and the power to carry that out."[5]

Imagine sustaining forward growth into higher states of consciousness and actions. Meditating with Jesus can guide us toward intimacy with divinity. We become more like those we spend time with, so why not spend time with Jesus? Jesus Christ, our brother and friend, can show us the way. This book and practice are for those who seek to know God better and, in doing so, are open to gaining self-awareness and wisdom. The result should be more happiness, peace, and joy.

The goal is to join the movement many are already on to ignite and empower the light within our hearts. We can do this through Christ-centered meditation and prayer. However, we must use our words and say, "I will move toward the light, and I trust that it will be beneficial for me and for others." This can cultivate the virtue of trust inside all of us.

INTEGRATE

Imagine having a wise friend who wants to know you and cocreate something special with you. With that in mind, commit to turning your attention to God's care and affection for a period every day. Spend more time focused on spiritual practices, spiritual and scriptural texts, relationships, and, above all else, the spirit of God, who is in your heart.

Get your mind used to the idea that meditating with Jesus will be beneficial. Notice any resistance. Ask Jesus to be closer to you and guide you into more truth. Or start wherever you are and be open to divine guidance. Seek truth above all else, and let truth find you. Keep your mind *and* heart open.

INQUIRY

1. What does your mind immediately resist most? Is it God, Jesus, meditation, transformation, surrender, or the search for your authentic purpose? Write down the words and thoughts that come with it. Can you accept that you have this resistance? Can you be okay with not knowing what it means?

2. Do you believe there is value in meditation? Why or why not?

3. Do you want to learn what you need from meditation and then use it, or do you see yourself becoming a lifetime meditator, going to deeper and deeper realms?

4. What are your fears about mediation, about getting closer to Jesus or exploring your body, soul, and spirit?

"The investment of one's life in others and the alignment of one's self with the forces that lead up and on—this does not come cheap. Once you go into it you're bound. You'll never be able to give it up. You'll find this furnishes your motive power. It will obsess you. Believe me: it'll be a magnificent obsession."[6] (Otto Kruger)

5. Do you believe in a higher power such as God, the universe, or spirituality? Write down your beliefs and doubts.

6. What is the name you call this higher power?

7. What are your goals for meditation? Is it improving your health and well-being, drawing closer to God, gaining more personal power, increasing your focus and concentration, or decreasing anxiety or depression?

8. Do you believe you have the power to be a cocreator with God? If not, why? Is this a limited belief that you may need to let go of? If so, what new thought can you use as a personal mantra?

"I pray that out of his glorious riches he may strengthen you with power through his Spirit in your inner being, so that Christ may dwell in your hearts through faith. And I pray that you, being rooted and established in love, may have power, together with all the Lord's holy people, to grasp how wide and long and high and deep is the love of Christ, and to know this love that surpasses knowledge—that you may be filled to the measure of all the fullness of God." (Ephesians 3:16–19 NIV)

DAILY PRACTICE—RESTORE

Be still, and know that I am God! I will be honored by
every nation. I will be honored throughout the world.

—Psalm 46:10 NLV

Daily spiritual practices bring us home to our hearts. Love is restored and perfected in us as we learn to be still, meditate, and surrender to knowing and honoring God, who is love. Meditating with Jesus takes time and discipline yet establishes an unshakable relationship of trust in ourselves and God's higher powers. Every day, we gain a new perspective with a bigger picture, enabling us to let go of the past and the limited ways we might be living. It can feel like being born again as a new person each day.

Jesus said, "Here's what I want you to do: Find a quiet, secluded place so you won't be tempted to role-play before God. Just be there as simply and honestly as you can manage"

(Matthew 6:6 MSG). As easy as this sounds, it's not. Finding a quiet place takes effort. Being alone with *ourselves*—our minds, emotions, and desires—as honestly as we can might be something new or terrifying or not fun. The trick is to be willing to try getting to know who we are—the most honest, real, and vulnerable version of ourselves. We might be surprised at how much love and goodness exist inside us.

Meditation is the daily practice of becoming still to explore and restore our inner lives. It takes us from the outer world of distraction, busyness, pleasure, and pursuit and aligns us with the life and virtues of God, such as hope, faithfulness, and wisdom. We begin to know God's spirit and how it intimately works in us, for us, and around us. We begin to see, know, and understand God. When we routinely become conscious and aware of God's spirit in our hearts, the natural outcome is healing and restoration of strength within our bodies.

The best way to begin is to establish a secluded place to meet with God daily, where we can learn to listen for and tell the truth. In stillness, we can find and explore the different aspects of our unique souls and experience a powerful force that ignites inner transformation. When we do, we can form an honest relationship with ourselves. It is a process of discovery, attention, and listening, which are forms of self-love. And love is power. Therefore, it should be no surprise that Jesus was anointed to help others deepen the love and understanding of their human *and* divine nature.

When we repeatedly return to our hearts—connecting to Christ's light, life, and love—we activate a higher power. This results in our ability to accept all that we are and everything happening in the present moment without fear or judgment and remain in a state of love, peace, and compassion. Through this process, we can become more grateful for the insights we receive and learn to live with what is true for us.

INTROSPECTION

A perfect haircut, a fit body, a smile for everyone, and a big lie in my heart—attempting perfection was my defense. I was out of control, but I dared not tell anyone.

When alone, cracks appeared in my armor. I couldn't hold in the overflowing pain of my childhood traumas, unexpressed resentments, and many false beliefs. Severe dysfunction manifested in my behavior and life. My heart was broken and closed. Yet I put on the mask and went out smiling. I was stuck in a cycle of fear. I was always in fight-or-flight mode, and I usually chose flight. I intuited that I had a peaceful spirit but couldn't get close to it because my soul was overactive and distressed. I needed to run, starve, binge, numb, act, and keep up appearances.

I tried to meditate for years, even before I had my full-blown anxiety disorder, yet a current of fear was always beneath the surface. I couldn't do it. I would only sit still for about three minutes and then be off. I had things to do!

I kept trying, and as I learned to endure and persist in stillness during meditation, God became a real presence, guiding me into a life where I experience my losses *and* victories, my blessings *and* challenges, my dark *and* light. I became grounded in acceptance, peace, and love. Every day is now a gift to explore who I am and who God is. I'm forever grateful to have found my soul and the spirit of God within my heart.

My relationship with Jesus continued to grow. Jesus is all about light, calling himself the "light of the world" (John 8:12 ESV). He taught me how to not remain in darkness. I discovered how to use the divine spark of light in my heart to shine on the dark, hidden, and repressed thoughts, emotions, and desires buried deep in my soul. This daily practice helped me purify my heart and keep it open so I could continue to see God at work inside me and in my life. Little by little, my old anxieties and fears were released. My inner transformation became the power I needed to transform my outer life.

At some point, I needed to go inward, overcome the obstacle of resistance, and set my darkness free to make room for more light. It happened because God is gentle, never giving me what I couldn't handle. I learned that going within is not that hard and not that bad. It's actually freeing, and it became enjoyable, almost blissful, once I spent the time to learn and appreciate the process. Plus, it became rewarding. Whenever I delved deeper, I received more of God's powerful light, life, and love. Slowly, I loved myself more, loved others more, and loved my life more.

INSIGHT

Jesus woke up early and went to a private place to meditate and pray. He taught his followers by example how he needed time alone to talk to and hear from his Father. He became still so that he could focus his attention on God's presence. This routine practice enabled him to become restored with the life and power of God's spirit and simultaneously have his heart renewed with wisdom, light, and love.

A daily practice of reconciling our truth with God's truth, learning to accept and allow all we find, will purify and open our hearts, bringing an increased flow of energy and creativity. Our hearts are the center of spiritual activity, where we learn who God is and who we are—separate yet connected identities. All of us are joined as one spirit with God and one another. Becoming more intimate with God helps us learn to listen with kindness and respect and communicate gently and lovingly to ourselves and others.

People talk casually about "doing the work" of becoming awakened or enlightened. The work is done on the inner person. This is why we dedicate time to going inward and healing ourselves through attention and compassion, to finding our unique voices and perhaps our destinies. By doing this daily, we develop a sense of well-being that comes from within. It may bring a simple smile or a peaceful or kind gesture, but we find that we give more of ourselves to life. We have less fear and more courage and curiosity. The mystery in and around us becomes a beautiful and interesting journey.

We gain a deeper sense of who we are and who we are meant to be. We let go of what we no longer need, who we are not, and who we are not meant to be with. We start wherever we are, however we are, and this process repeats itself over and over. Along the way, we find lost parts of ourselves, such as innocence, peace, and happiness.

When we learn to honor and value everything we find in our souls, we practice self-love because our souls *are* our selves. We also learn to surrender ourselves to the perfection and wisdom of God's spirit. We realize powerful forces are inside and around us. Being aware of this helps us become more discerning and better able to make wise decisions that will benefit ourselves and others.

INSPIRATION

We can establish new pathways between the soul and heart, bringing us wholeness and integrity. When this occurs, our inner lives transform. Where there was once chaos, there exists only calm. Instead of confusion, there is clarity. We become intimate and honest with

Tonyah Dee

God, which leads to greater intimacy with ourselves. Ultimately, this can help us in all our relationships.

As we deepen our relationship with Christ, we recover faith and trust in ourselves and God, both of which we may have lost along the way or never have known. Our inner and outer lives become an expansion of all that God is. We receive the subtle power to be patient, kind, gentle, and honest. We gain self-control, allowing us to spend our energy building the lives of our dreams and serving others or the planet.

Once we ignite the light within our hearts, known as the spirit of truth, we are led into more light, which represents new life. Change always starts with the truth. One main goal of meditating with Jesus is to befriend and surrender our souls and become receptive to God's spirit of truth as he leads us into more light, into becoming enlightened. Learning to honor truth brings us integrity within our bodies, souls, and spirits, leading to inner strength.

The unconditional love of Christ is accessible to everyone. We can become more like Jesus, able to remain in peace and love others no matter the circumstances. This helps us to live a life of being in the kingdom of God while here on earth. As Jesus said, "Neither will they say, 'Look, here!' or, 'Look, there!' for behold, God's Kingdom is within you" (Luke 17:21 WEB).

This step is about reconciling our relationship with God—our intimate, caring parent—to restore our hearts and lives. It is very important to know there's no right or wrong way to be still with God. Every day will be different. One of the biggest challenges is returning to our space and allowing what is true. Spiritual awakening takes time, and spiritual disciplines can speed up the process. I always feel better after time spent communing with God.

The goal is to stay connected to stability, be restored by love, and be guided by the voice of God. This can cultivate the virtue of faithfulness inside all of us.

INTEGRATE

Create a space, a "God spot," where you can be alone with God. Try establishing a morning routine. For example, set your alarm, shower, and then meditate. Decide in advance how you will sit. Will you use a chair, cushion, or couch?

Have your favorite devotional chant or hymn music accessible. In addition, have this workbook, a Bible, a journal, a pencil, and a music source nearby. I also keep a place for my coffee, singing bowls, and favorite devotionals in my dedicated meditation and prayer spot. Lighting a candle or incense can signify that you are entering a sacred space.

Experiment with your best time to practice. Give early morning a chance, as Jesus did, so that you can start your day being filled with God's grace.

Resist the temptation to skip the practice. Instead, show up for yourself. There's no judgment. There's no right way or right amount of time. Most of all, make the experience enjoyable.

If you follow these simple steps, day by day, you can be transformed, cleansed, and purified according to God's design and purpose.

INQUIRY

1. What did it feel like to create or designate for yourself a personal space to meet with God?

2. Do you think you can continue to return each day and observe your soul in an honest and vulnerable way? Why or why not? What scares you the most? Can you be okay with not meditating perfectly?

3. How does it feel to be a beginner, to learn something new? Are you excited? Is it a drag? Or is it both?

4. What is your biggest vision for your life? If you don't know yet, what is the dream that you have?

"To be yourself in a world that is constantly trying to make you something else is the greatest accomplishment."[7] (Ralph Waldo Emerson)

Tonyah Dee

5. Who are you? Name five of your top values.

6. Are you living these values? What do you need to focus more on?

7. Can you commit to being nonjudgmental and more accepting of yourself?

8. Do you have a daily morning routine? An evening routine? If not, what would be your ideal routines in the morning and night?

"Finally, brothers and sisters, rejoice! Strive for full restoration, encourage one another, be of one mind, live in peace. And the God of love and peace will be with you." (2 Corinthians 13:11 NIV)

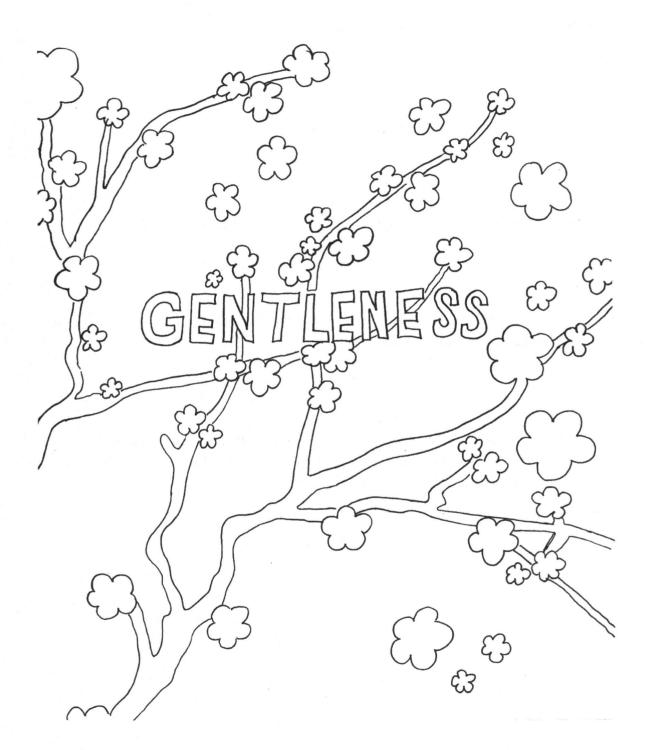

THE BODY—SANCTUARY

THE BODY

Gentleness

> Or do you not know that your body is a temple of the Holy Spirit
> within you, whom you have from God? You are not your own.
> —1 Corinthians 6:19 ESV

The first higher power is establishing a daily practice, and the second is knowing and being fully present in your body. There is no perfect body or person, but everybody is the temple and home of God's perfect spirit. Each of us lives in a body, has a soul, and *is* a spirit. We have a human spirit designed to connect to God's spirit in our hearts. This is the completeness of our being; we have a physical, psychological, and spiritual self. When we turn our attention to our bodies, we discover parts of ourselves we may have disconnected from or are unfamiliar with.

Take the soul, for example. Like a computer hard drive, the soul records and stores everything we've learned and experienced. Sometimes for our health and well-being, we may need to go in and empty the trash. Meditation is a way to receive God's powerful purification program, which eliminates viruses of the mind and helps us to decipher what needs to go and what needs to stay.

Besides physical activity, many psychological and spiritual activities go on inside our bodies. During meditation, we reacquaint ourselves with our unique body, soul, and spirit *and* get to know God's spirit. We tap into the wisdom trying to guide us. The body can thus become a sanctuary of safety, where we gently become grounded in the here and now, listening for insightful messages. The body is a messenger; it speaks.

Unfortunately, we often mistreat our bodies to ignore or numb physical or psychological pain. We blindly and unconsciously act out the erratic desires, pangs of hunger, and impulses of our souls, which may lead to feelings of shame, guilt, or grief. This can cause us to overthink as we try to find solutions to our self-sabotage or suffering. Our bodies can become burdened, tired, scared, and emotionally full. Our hearts can become hardened or cold, unable to feel and hear the cry of our souls in the dark and in need of attention. This is traumatic in every sense of the word.

Meditating with Jesus creates the opposite experience. When we meditate with Jesus, we teach ourselves to be kind and gentle and to listen, understand, value, and accept our unique bodies and souls. We connect to God's stability and unconditional love in the center of our hearts. We sit in this love in our bodies. After repeatedly engaging with this practice, we attain the ability to be with ourselves, embodied, meaning taking and settling our attention inward to connect to the presence and aliveness of our being. We learn to do this moment to moment without having reactions that could lead to negative consequences. We learn to endure the agony of the human experience *and* experience the beauty of it simultaneously. This pattern of acceptance and nonreaction becomes a new habit, which always benefits us.

Embracing who we are in this way changes how our souls feel; and new life, along with new healthier emotions, comes flowing through our hearts, healing and restoring us with a deep sense of gratitude for taking this time to value ourselves. If we can learn to sit still in our bodies and practice self-control and patience, these qualities grow; and we can then take these virtues out into our day. God's spirit is inside our hearts, helping us to bear witness to our struggles. The result is that we feel united with something larger than ourselves. A shift from feeling powerless to feeling powerful occurs, allowing us to move forward to experience new ways of being and, hopefully, enjoy new revelations.

INTROSPECTION

I ran when I felt something I didn't want to feel. I starved myself when I needed something more. I numbed when I couldn't face my reality. Hello, my name is Tonyah; and I abused, neglected, and abandoned my body for years. When I finally stopped running or numbing from the painful thoughts, emotions, and desires inside my body and learned to turn toward them, I recovered from many strange behaviors.

My soul was severely wounded when, at fourteen, I returned home from a summer vacation to learn my mother had moved out without a word. Over the following months, my family disintegrated, and I was left alone. My once safe and happy place became a ghost town with dead plants and disappearing objects. My friends, the ones living out scary stories of their own, became my distraction. This new life was the beginning of my demise as I slowly lost myself, and all that I had once known and cherished disappeared.

That year, as I forged forward from being a teen to a young woman, my godfather sexually violated me. In that same short season, on a summer night after a concert with my friends, I was in a car accident where I flew out the windshield, breaking my back. I was millimeters away from being paralyzed. This last shock established a foundation of fear and pain on all levels—body, soul, and spirit. I was broken and brokenhearted. I was in the hospital for a while; and afterward, I moved houses and changed schools several times.

Because of these traumas, I felt alone, scared, and lost during most of my teens and young adulthood. My soul was full of fear, anger, hurt, and distrust. I established in my mind the negative thought I wasn't valued or wanted and that people can and will betray me. I became certain I could not depend on anyone. Fixed false thoughts caused me to isolate, run, and numb.

I stored these thoughts, feelings, and beliefs in my soul, and they became the barometer that navigated my life for many years. The outcome of believing these thoughts kept me afraid and insecure. I took my body for granted for many years, even unconsciously punishing it for carrying so much pain inside me. Unable to tolerate my feelings, I attempted to throw them up, starve them, run away from them, and employ various other avoidance strategies.

I slowly realized the only way through pain was to enter it and shine the light of truth and compassion. In doing so, I began to accept the pain, go into the darkness, face my reality, and seek the light. This took me to the other side where I was liberated and set free. I must say it's nice to have a practice that teaches me how to do this right inside my body.

For many years, I thought I couldn't trust anyone because of the harm done, but the truth was that I couldn't trust myself. I was like them—abusive and neglectful but only to myself, to my soul. It has taken me years to love my body *and* what's inside of it. Once I received God's spirit through faith in Christ, I heard a new and different voice. One of acceptance, compassion, and love.

After years of counseling others on how to use food to feed the body, I had the epiphany of how important it is to feed my body, soul, *and* spirit to have deep, enduring, and sustainable change. Meditation is like a detox diet to my soul, releasing stored toxins and feeding it with attention and compassion. This daily practice nourishes and sustains me. And, at the same time, my spirit is fed because it gets to do its job of elevating, magnifying, and transforming my soul to be its best self.

Turns out attention is an essential nutrient of love. My body held on to my pain until I paid attention to it. When I fed it compassion, my body let the pain go. My spirit has needs too. It feels complete and nourished when it is one with the Creator because where there is more spirit, there is more life.

I'm still learning to feed my body, soul, and spirit. Every day, I have the power to turn these parts of myself into a sanctuary of love, not hate. Peace begins with me. I realize I can choose every day to seek a higher truth, accept it, and surrender my pain and challenges to make the best choices possible. I'm not alone. I'm connected to life itself, evidenced by how my peace or anger has a ripple effect.

Balance and harmony are restored when I feed my body, soul, and spirit, allowing me to gracefully and consciously make positive decisions that affect my health and well-being.

Tonyah Dee

Through Christ-centered meditation and prayer, I've learned to work on loving *all* parts of myself.

INSIGHT

The body is the house of six senses; eleven organ systems; our soul (which includes the mind, emotions, and will); our human spirit; our conscience; our heart; and God's spirit. As you can tell, *a lot* goes on in our temple at any time! Unsurprisingly, among our *inner* parts, integrity and harmony are crucial for good physical, psychological, and spiritual health. We're complex beings. We're sensitive and strong. We can reason, have emotion, and seek out our desires. We know we are more than a body.

Awareness of our multidimensional nature signifies a deep sense that we are at home in our bodies. This awareness increases our ability to be in the present moment and be mindful of the sensations coming from our physical, psychological, and spiritual parts. During meditation and stillness, we strive to become comfortable in the sanctuary of our bodies, where we can begin an adventurous journey that leads us to our hearts, out of which all things flow. We can find a powerful source of light, love, and healing here if we are open to it. God's spirit—known by many names, including the spirit of Christ—is at our very core.

The body exists in the here and now. It cannot go back into the past or the future. Learning to be still and embodied gives us time to experience who we are in the present moment. This is where meditation can be difficult because our souls store past and current thoughts, emotions, and desires. The mind can think about the past or plan for the future. Our souls can distract us from the present and push us into a cycle of past and future.

However, when we make our bodies into a sanctuary, God's spirit can become our guide, whereupon he can lead us toward healing our souls and recovering our ability to remain peaceful in the reality of the present moment. We can awaken to the truth of who we are, which is like Jesus—human *and* divine. We are supernatural, unlike any other creature on this earth; and we can go deeper into the realms of truth, intuition, imagination, and creation, which is life-expanding. We have the power to change and adapt. We can expand our lives into new areas of possibility.

The negative can be safely subtracted from us and the positive added to us. We can leave behind fear, pain, doubt, shame, and insecurity and gain peace, strength, and freedom. We can gain an enhanced awareness and an ability to listen deeply and make better choices. We experience inner transformation. We can get on the path to wisdom. Our thoughts, emotions, and actions can change. When this happens, others notice. We notice.

INSPIRATION

When asked which is the greatest commandment, "Jesus replied, 'Love the Lord your God with all your heart and with all your soul and with all your mind.' This is the first and greatest commandment. And the second is like it: 'Love your neighbor as yourself'" (Matthew 22:37–39 NIV).

Jesus teaches us how to love. In meditation, we realize God is alive in our bodies. The result is that when we set out to love God with all our hearts, souls, and minds, the love inside of us increases. As love inside of us grows, it becomes easier to love others.

Little by little, layers of our old selves, the way we used to think and treat our bodies, fade away as the God-sized hole, the void within, is filled with the light, life, and love of Christ. Through this transformation, we begin to love ourselves. We begin to experience the peace and feeling of wholeness our bodies and souls long for. We experience an inner awareness of our dignity and worth.

Through meditation, we can find our true and hidden selves; and by accepting both, we realize, with God's help, that we are our own divine healers. There are no good or bad parts, no right or wrong, only truth. We are not just our own, but we are also of God. We learn to recognize his voice *and* our voice. This is satisfying and empowering. It is a victory we can use to overcome blockages and obstacles as we gain self-control over our minds, emotions, desires, actions, and reactions.

Our bodies are where this is happening. Our lives become our own science and research projects. We discover a newfound power to create ourselves, leading us to understand that we are always self-creating. This is a big contrast to life without Christ-centered meditation when we didn't have power over our choices.

Tonyah Dee

We can find creative power each time we consciously connect to a higher power. Every time we meditate with Jesus, we learn to create more goodness and kindness, more peace and joy, more love and patience. We go inward to explore our inner parts—body soul, and spirit—and learn to focus on God's spirit. In meditation, we try to become relaxed yet alert. This helps us walk through life calmly, with our eyes and hearts open. We can then focus on our dreams and God's plan for us.

The goals are to be present with our bodies and their inner parts, make a sanctuary for our souls, spirits, and God's spirit, be embodied, meaning listen to the messages within as our bodies speak to us, be present with the unconditional love in our hearts, and honor and value our bodies, knowing we are the host to God's supernatural divine spirit. This can cultivate the virtue of gentleness inside all of us.

INTEGRATE

Create a sanctuary in your body. Gently become as still as possible in a seated position. Your spine should be straight and your sitting bones stable. Your shoulders should be back, your heart open, and your chin tucked in. The top of your head should reach upward, and your belly should be soft.

Now imagine a cross from heaven to earth and shoulder to shoulder running through your body. Next, find a position of dignity. Close your eyes so you can direct your attention to explore your inner world.

Breathe slowly and deeply. Relax. Begin to experience your body as a temple of God's spirit, where you can experience God's presence and know your true nature.

Witness and observe your soul (your thoughts, feelings, and desires), yet be present and rooted in your heart. Resist the temptation to do this a certain way or force anything. Just be still in your temple as honestly as you can as you learn to witness who you are in that moment.

Hold this posture throughout the practice while remembering to breathe fully, calmly, and stay relaxed. Learn to become still, peaceful, and relaxed for three minutes, then five, then ten, etc., as you continue to practice daily.

Tonyah Dee

HUMAN BEING

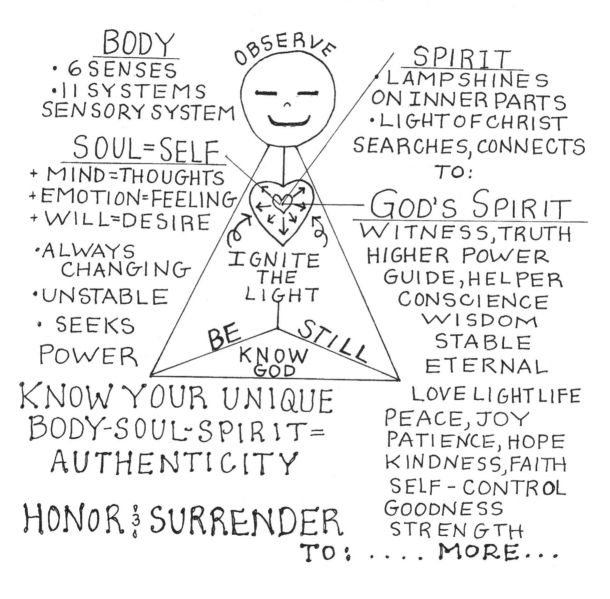

BODY
- 6 SENSES
- 11 SYSTEMS
SENSORY SYSTEM

OBSERVE

SPIRIT
- LAMP SHINES ON INNER PARTS
- LIGHT OF CHRIST SEARCHES, CONNECTS TO:

SOUL = SELF
+ MIND = THOUGHTS
+ EMOTION = FEELING
+ WILL = DESIRE
- ALWAYS CHANGING
- UNSTABLE
- SEEKS POWER

IGNITE THE LIGHT

BE STILL
KNOW GOD

GOD'S SPIRIT
WITNESS, TRUTH
HIGHER POWER
GUIDE, HELPER
CONSCIENCE
WISDOM
STABLE
ETERNAL

LOVE LIGHT LIFE
PEACE, JOY
PATIENCE, HOPE
KINDNESS, FAITH
SELF - CONTROL
GOODNESS
STRENGTH
TO: .... MORE...

KNOW YOUR UNIQUE
BODY-SOUL-SPIRIT=
AUTHENTICITY

HONOR ¾ SURRENDER

INQUIRY

1. Was there a time when you really enjoyed being in your body? What age were you? What did you enjoy?

2. How are you now with your body? Do you turn toward or away from it when it hurts?

3. Do you find yourself criticizing your body? Judging? What exactly are you saying to yourself?

4. Did someone in your earlier life say these same things?

"Real liberation comes not from glossing over or repressing painful states of feeling, but only from experiencing them to the full."[8] (Carl Jung)

Tonyah Dee

5. How have you abandoned, rejected, or abused your body? Did someone earlier or does someone now cause you to feel these emotions?

6. Are you willing to forgive yourself and start a new relationship with your body?

7. How can you create a safe place for your body and emotions?

8. How can you love your body more?

"I will give thanks to you, for I am fearfully and wonderfully made. Your works are wonderful. My soul knows that very well." (Psalm 139:14 WEB)

THE BREATH—CREATE

THE BREATH

> The Spirit of God has made me, And the breath
> of the Almighty gives me life.
>
> —Job 33:4 NASB

The first thing we do as we come into this world is take a breath. We inhale, and life begins. An exhale is the last thing we do before passing. It is that simple: breath equals life. Staying aware of our breath and how we are breathing is a higher power we can all learn with a little practice.

Some believe the breath is God's spirit because of the ways it can be defined. The root word for breath is *spiritus*, which also means spirit, vitality, courage, power, and inspiration.[9] The breath is a link that unites our bodies, souls, and spirits with God's spirit as it moves and flows freely into and out of us, empowering every cell with life.

We can learn to use the breath of life as a healing force to create inner calm, serenity, and new pathways to our hearts. Doctors, meditation facilitators, and stress-reduction teachers use deep-breathing techniques for healing and stress reduction[10] because slow rhythmic breathing releases a relaxation response throughout the body, initiating healing and renewal.

Holding the breath or shallow breathing releases stress hormones and causes disease in the body.[11] Fortunately, we can affect our health and well-being positively. With that in mind, relax, inhale a deep breath all the way to your tummy, let it expand, and then exhale slowly. Smile. Do you feel better?

The way we breathe can improve or cause distress in our lives. The breath calms or causes anxiety in our bodies and works on relaxing or exciting the nervous system. When we are in a state of stress or chaos, we can learn to use our breath as a centering force, first by taking long, slow, deep breaths. That's why so many meditation practices begin with conscious breathing.

How we breathe directly affects our physical health and well-being. How we breathe can change the electric currents cycling in the brain known as brain waves.[12] Meditation and breathwork can retrain the brain to produce brain waves that increase creativity, cause a deep, peaceful state, and bring our bodies into balance and harmony.

Breath brings new life and makes us come alive. If we want even more power, we can turn to God's spirit. We all have this incredible opportunity to be born again over and over to become a new person daily (or moment to moment). When we consciously use our breath and words to invite the love of Christ to grow in our hearts, the breath of life flows in, and we receive.

We can use our breath to do so many things for us. Consider using it to float our words into the universe by saying, "I want you" or "I need you." Because God is in the very air that surrounds us, our messages will be heard. God faithfully and lovingly breathes back his life and peace into us. It is as easy as that. Ask and receive. Jesus said, "'Peace be to you. As the Father has sent me, even so I send you.' When he had said this, he breathed on them, and said to them, 'Receive the Holy Spirit'" (John 20:21–22 WEB)

INTROSPECTION

I had no voice left. It had disappeared from barely being used and hardly ever heard. Only after eight years of talk therapy did I realize my childhood had caused me to hold my tongue, never wanting to cause waves. This was a great way for me to give away my power. I did it because I lacked good communication skills and feared being hurt. I wasn't taught to express my truthful words or shown the importance of knowing my authentic and unique soul—my thoughts, feelings, and desires. Without realizing it, I let myself be vulnerable to people who knew what they wanted and could easily use their words to meet their needs.

It's not surprising that over the years, I've been attracted to charming people who knew how to use words to please, manipulate, or control me. Most likely, these people were never taught to be authentic and honest. Many times, I've said yes when I needed to say no. I've kept my mouth shut about knowing the truth. I've been unaware of when I was holding my breath around a person or a situation, or I've failed to notice my breathing was shallow out of fear.

My communication skills changed once I learned how to monitor, observe, and respect my breath while meditating. I was more aware of when I became uncomfortable or triggered around certain people or situations. Instead of reacting, I would focus on slowly breathing in through my nose and exhaling long, relaxed breaths. Because of this exercise, I could remain still and silent yet present and alert. It was as if my breath created a natural boundary of safety, giving me the time to calm my soul and go deeper into a place of wisdom. It gave me the time to listen not just from my ears but also from my heart.

As I've gained self-control and, with it, strength, I can respond honestly and calmly. Instead of reacting harshly and impulsively or only taking care of the other person's needs, I take care of my needs as well. I use compassionate words, such as "Sounds like you're really stressed. I'll pray for you." I use words to establish boundaries, like "No, thank you, I'm not interested in that." I am kind and clear with people and am comfortable saying, "I don't think we are interested in the same things or have the same values."

My breath connects me to God's spirit. This power is the shield that gives me a chance, an opportunity, to pause so I can connect to a place of inner guidance, where wisdom and truth are. I do this from a place of love, not fear. Through inhaling and exhaling my breath consciously, I can control myself and allow my spirit to hear how much pain people are in or what they are asking of me. This gives me all the power I need to give them the very thing we all seek: to be heard, understood, valued, and, on some level, cared for and loved. Through my breath and voice, I've found my power.

At some point, I realized breath plus words equals a new positive life and fewer negative consequences. This practice was only the beginning of knowing how to love others and myself. It was through becoming still and meditating with Jesus that I learned to observe my breathing and connect to God's spirit, calming my soul enough so I could listen and speak wisely. This life experience has since allowed me to bring conscious, relaxed deep breathing into other relationships. It has enabled and given me the practical tools to become a good listener and offer an empathetic ear to myself and others.

INSIGHT

The breath connects to God's Holy Spirit, which flows like wind and fire to purify our hearts and souls. The breath is a purifying, calming, detoxifying, and healing force we can use to change our chemical composition and regulate our nervous system. Through conscious breathing, we can create feelings of safety and serenity and a connection to our inner self while keeping an open ear and heart for someone else.

Being able to control and focus our breath also helps us control our actions. The breath is a source of power that gives us a chance when triggered or confused to pause and seek the wisdom of God. When incited, have a strong craving, feel offended, or have a powerful emotional reaction to a situation, we can turn our attention to our breathing as an immediate response to counterbalance the reaction. We can use the breath as a coping mechanism to ground ourselves and reroute our emotions to our hearts. Breath delivers us into the current of faith, where we can find a higher power.

Although the breathing process is primarily unconscious, it can be overridden by conscious command. Learning to direct the breath into a natural, relaxed rhythm is a powerful step to having an increased ability to return to a state of peace.

The first step is awareness. We must go from breathing unconsciously and paying no attention to our breath to having a consistent awareness of how we are breathing, especially during times of stress or psychological upset.

Tonyah Dee